Salads

GENERAL EDITOR
CHUCK WILLIAMS

RECIPES
EMANUELA STUCCHI PRINETTI

PHOTOGRAPHY
ALLAN ROSENBERG

TIME
LIFE
BOOKS

Time-Life Books is a division of
TIME LIFE INCORPORATED

President and CEO: John M. Fahey, Jr.
President, Time-Life Books: John D. Hall

TIME-LIFE CUSTOM PUBLISHING

Vice President and Publisher: Terry Newell
Sales Director: Frances C. Mangan
Editorial Director: Donia Steele

WILLIAMS-SONOMA
Founder/Vice-Chairman: Chuck Williams

WELDON OWEN INC.
President: John Owen
Publisher: Wendely Harvey
Managing Editor: Laurie Wertz
Consulting Editor: Norman Kolpas
Copy Editor: Sharon Silva
Editorial Assistant: Janique Poncelet
Design: John Bull, The Book Design Company
Production: Stephanie Sherman, James Obata,
    Mick Bagnato
Co-Editions Director: Derek Barton
Co-Editions Production Manager (US): Tarji Mickelson
Food Photographer: Allan Rosenberg
Additional Food Photography: Allen V. Lott
Primary Food & Prop Stylist: Sandra Griswold
Food Stylist: Heidi Gintner
Prop Assistant: Karen Nicks
Glossary Illustrations: Alice Harth

The Williams-Sonoma Kitchen Library
conceived and produced by Weldon Owen Inc.
814 Montgomery St., San Francisco, CA 94133

In collaboration with Williams-Sonoma
100 North Point, San Francisco, CA 94133

Production by Mandarin Offset, Hong Kong
Printed in China

A Note on Weights and Measures:
All recipes include customary U.S. and metric
measurements. Metric conversions are based on
a standard developed for these books and have
been rounded off. Actual weights may vary

A Weldon Owen Production

Copyright © 1993 Weldon Owen Inc.
Reprinted in 1993; 1993; 1993; 1995; 1995; 1995
All rights reserved, including the right of
reproduction in whole or in part in any form.

Library of Congress
Cataloging-in-Publication Data:

Salads / general editor, Chuck Williams ;
    recipes, Emanuela Stucchi Prinetti ;
    photography, Allan Rosenberg.
        p.   cm. — (Williams-Sonoma kitchen library)
    Includes index.
    ISBN 0-7835-0237-0 ;
    ISBN 0-7835-0238-9 (pbk.)
    1. Salads   I. Williams, Chuck.
    II. Prinetti, Emanuela Stucchi.   III. Series.
    TX740.S272   1993
    641.8'3—dc20   92-18191
                                    CIP

Contents

Appetizers 15

Main Courses 43

Accompaniments 67

Fruit Salads 97

INTRODUCTION

Nowadays, when we speak about good cooking we invariably single out the use of fresh ingredients. That is one reason why salads are so popular: Nothing you serve or eat could possibly look or taste fresher.

That freshness also carries with it the benefit of good health. We have a new awareness of how good for you foods from the garden can be—low in fat and calories, high in dietary fiber, rich with vitamins and minerals.

And, as this book demonstrates, salads have more variety than any other category of cooking. They can be served as casual or elegant appetizers or accompaniments, or a single salad can be an entire meal in itself. Virtually anything can go into a salad, in any combination: lettuces and other leaves, of course, and all kinds of vegetables and fruits; seafood, meats and poultry of every description; cheeses and eggs; and all manner of beans, pulses, grains and pastas.

You'll get a taste of all these ingredients in the 45 recipes featured in this book, each of which is accompanied by a full-color photograph to show you how the finished dish looks. You'll also find helpful guides to the fundamentals of salad making: a survey of the kitchen equipment you'll need; a simple demonstration of how to prepare and serve a perfect salad; and instructions for salad dressings that are so easy to make and so delicious that you'll never again need or want to use a bottled dressing. There's also an illustrated glossary of basic ingredients, which includes a guide to the salad leaves most commonly available in supermarkets and greengrocers. Above all, I hope this book shows you how absolutely simple salad making can be. Its goal is to inspire you to put a fresh, healthful, delicious salad on your own table today—and every day.

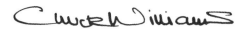

EQUIPMENT

Basic tools for cleaning, peeling, paring, cutting, dressing and serving salad ingredients

All the equipment you need to make most salads is a bowl and serving implements. But the few pieces of equipment shown here will make the work go more easily and ensure more attractive and flavorful results.

A salad spinner, for example, guarantees that no droplets of water will dilute a salad's dressing. And an array of cutting implements—basic kitchen knives, vegetable peelers, melon ballers, mandolines—speeds preparation and expands the cook's repertoire of decorative effects.

1. Mixing Bowls
Sturdy bowls in a range of sizes for mixing and serving salads and dressings. Can be made of earthenware, porcelain, glass or stainless steel.

2. Kitchen Towels
Cotton towels for patting salad leaves dry. May also be used for holding leaves, loosely rolled up, to crisp in the refrigerator.

3. Colander and Strainer
For washing and draining salad vegetables. Choose stainless steel; enameled-steel colanders are also good choices.

4. Molds
Fluted tinplate or stainless-steel molds hold gelatin salads and unmold easily. Available in large and small sizes.

5. Mandoline
Rapidly slices, shreds and juliennes vegetables; particularly good for shredding

cabbage. Select a model with detachable blades that offer a choice of cutting surfaces.

6. Lemon Juicer
For reaming lemon halves to obtain the small quantities of juice called for in some recipes.

7. Pepper Mill
Select a sturdy model with hardened-steel works that adjust to varying degrees of grind. Small side hatch on the cast-aluminum model shown enables easy filling.

8. Kitchen Scissors
For cutting up relatively small, light ingredients, including green (spring) onions, chives and parsley.

9. Garlic Press
For crushing fresh garlic cloves. Choose a model—usually cast aluminum—that feels comfortable in the hand and has a sturdy, durable hinge and

a plastic cleaning tool for unclogging the holes.

10. Salad Spinner
Geared mechanism inside the lid rapidly spins the colanderlike inner basket to remove water droplets from salad leaves by centrifugal force; water collects in spinner's outer receptacle.

11. Liquid Measuring Cups
For accurate measuring of liquid ingredients. Choose heavy-duty heat-resistant glass, marked on one side in cups and ounces and on the other in milliliters. Lip and handle allow for easy pouring.

12. Rotary Mincer
Rolled across a work surface, parallel circular stainless-steel blades quickly and neatly mince fresh herbs without crushing them and allow good control over fineness.

13. Egg Wedger
Cupped end of hinged stainless-steel tool holds a shelled hard-cooked egg; when tool is closed, crossed wires cut 6 neat wedges.

14. Melon Ball Scoop
Sharp-edged stainless-steel scoop cuts neat balls of melon and other soft fruits and vegetables for attractive presentation.

15. Vegetable Peelers
Curved slotted swiveling blade thinly strips away the peel from carrots and other root vegetables, and is also useful for thinly paring citrus zests.

Available in models with blades set either parallel or perpendicular to handle; choose whichever type feels most comfortable to you.

16. Measuring Spoons
In graduated sizes, for measuring small quantities of ingredients. To assure accurate measurements, choose good-quality, calibrated metal spoons with deep bowls.

17. Table Fork
For stirring small quantities of salad dressing.

18. Chef's Knife and Paring Knife
The larger chef's knife chops and slices large items or large quantities of ingredients; the smaller paring knife peels vegetables and cuts up small ingredients. Choose sturdy knives with sharp, stainless-steel blades securely attached to sturdy handles that feel comfortable in the hand.

19. Wire Strainer
Small, fine-meshed strainer for straining lemon juice or dressings. May also be used to skim vegetables from water after blanching or parboiling.

20. Salad Servers
Oversized spoon and fork efficiently toss salad ingredients with dressing. Though made in a wide range of materials, wood surfaces grip ingredients better for serving.

21. Wire Whisks
For stirring salad dressings in large or small quantities.

SALAD BASICS

Simple tips to ensure a fresh, crisp, attractive and flavorful salad

No recipe could seem simpler than placing a few lettuce leaves in a bowl, tossing them with a dressing and serving. In truth, that sums up how easily most salads are prepared. But a little extra attention to detail can make the difference between a limp, tasteless salad and one that is attractive, crisp and flavorful.

Begin by selecting the freshest, best-quality salad leaves you can find—crisp and bright, with no signs of wilting or discoloration (see the glossary, page 106, for a guide to some of the most commonly available greens). Wash them thoroughly but gently to remove all dirt. This step is particularly important with spinach leaves, which may require several changes of water to eliminate all traces of the sandy soil in which they grow. Dry your salad greens with just as much diligence; water left clinging to the leaves will dilute the flavor of the dressing.

Pay attention to the way you prepare the leaves for the salad bowl. All too often, home cooks fail to tear the leaves into pieces small enough to be eaten in a single bite, turning one of the simplest of one-fork dishes into an awkward eating experience.

Whatever goes into your salad, in most cases it should be dressed and tossed just moments before serving. Prolonged contact with the dressing will cause leaves to wilt. Notable exceptions are recipes in which the dressing is deliberately used to change the texture or flavor of the ingredients through marination.

1. Separating the leaves.
One by one, break whole lettuce leaves—in this case, romaine (cos) lettuce—from their core. Alternatively, grasp the core firmly at its base; twist sharply and pull to break it away from all the leaves.

2. Washing the leaves.
Swish the leaves in a bowl, basin or sink of cold water to remove any dirt. If they are very dirty, as spinach leaves sometimes are, lift them out, drain and rinse the receptacle; repeat the process until no dirt remains. Alternatively, wash individual leaves under cold running water.

3. Spin drying.
To eliminate water droplets that would dilute dressings, put the leaves in a salad spinner and pull or turn the handle; pour off water from the outer bowl and repeat until no water remains. Alternatively, arrange the leaves in a single layer between two kitchen towels and pat dry.

4. Crisping the leaves.
If you want crisp, cold salad leaves, arrange them in a single layer on a clean, damp kitchen towel. Gently roll up the towel and refrigerate for at least 1 hour.

5. Tearing the leaves.
To prepare the salad for serving, use your fingers to tear each leaf into irregular bite-sized pieces, tossing them directly into the salad bowl.

6. Cutting shreds.
If a recipe calls for shredded lettuce, neatly stack several leaves on a cutting surface. With a sharp knife, cut across the leaves to make strips of the desired width.

7. Dressing the salad.
Add other salad ingredients and garnishes—in this case, croutons, Parmesan shavings, capers and anchovies. Just before serving, prepare the dressing and pour it over the salad.

8. Tossing the salad.
Using a pair of salad servers or two large spoons or forks, turn the salad ingredients over and over in the bowl, until they are all evenly coated with the dressing.

VINAIGRETTES

Highlighting the fresh taste of a salad with a basic blend of oil and vinegar or lemon juice

The simplest form of salad dressing is vinaigrette, a French term meaning "little vinegar" that describes any blend of vinegar or lemon juice and oil. That basic formula can yield myriad flavorful dressings—including the three recipes on the right—to complement any salad you prepare.

Vinegar, resulting from a secondary fermentation of wine or cider, contributes the characteristics of the liquid from which it was made. Red wine vinegar tastes more robust than one derived from white wine, and cider vinegar displays the sweet, tart flavor of apples. Lemon juice, with a similar level of acidity, adds its own fresh, bright taste.

Oil helps the dressing coat the salad ingredients. Aromatic, fruity olive oil is the classic choice. Other oils, such as walnut, sunflower seed and sesame seed, contribute their own distinctive flavor to a salad.

Simple Vinaigrette

A dressing should enhance and harmonize with the simple, fresh tastes of a salad. For this reason, close attention to the quality of ingredients is of utmost importance. Extra-virgin olive oil, made from the first cold pressing of the fruit, is the best choice. The vinegar should be made from good-quality red or white wine. This recipe makes enough to dress ¾–1 pound (400–500 g) of greens, which will serve 6 people.

salt
1 tablespoon red or white wine vinegar
¼ cup (2 fl oz/60 ml) extra-virgin olive oil

*P*lace salt to taste in a small bowl. Add the vinegar and stir with a fork until completely dissolved. Add the oil and stir vigorously until well blended.

Makes about 6 tablespoons (3 fl oz/90 ml)

1. Dissolving the salt.
Before pouring in any oil (which would prevent salt from dissolving), combine the salt with the vinegar or, as shown here, lemon juice. Stir until the salt is completely dissolved.

2. Mixing in the oil.
Slowly pour in the oil, stirring briskly to emulsify the dressing—suspending droplets of oil in the acidic liquid. In most cases, 4 parts oil is used for each part vinegar or lemon juice.

3. Adding herbs.
If you want to add extra flavor and color, stir in finely chopped fresh herbs to taste. Pour the vinaigrette over the salad and toss well.

Herb Vinaigrette

This dressing is good on cooked vegetables such as potatoes, carrots, zucchini or fennel. Vary the herbs to create different flavor combinations. For example, use thyme, oregano and mint for a true Mediterranean taste. Minced fennel seeds are also an interesting addition. Fresh herbs are preferable, as their aroma is stronger; however, dried herbs can be used, halving the quantities.

salt
1 tablespoon fresh lemon juice
¼ cup (2 fl oz/60 ml) extra-virgin olive oil
1 teaspoon minced fresh parsley
1 teaspoon minced fresh tarragon
1 teaspoon minced fresh chives

Place salt to taste in a small bowl. Add the lemon juice and stir with a fork until completely dissolved. Add the oil and stir vigorously until well blended. Then stir in the herbs and mix well.

Makes about ⅓ cup (3 fl oz/80 ml)

Country Dressing

A simple tossed salad of radicchio, romaine (cos) lettuce and arugula (rocket) mates well with this full-bodied dressing. For a more aromatic blend, use balsamic vinegar in place of the red wine vinegar. The quantity of garlic you use depends upon how strong a garlic flavor you prefer. Start with a little and add more until the taste pleases you.

2 cloves garlic, thinly sliced or passed through a
  garlic press
1 tablespoon honey
salt
1 tablespoon red wine vinegar or balsamic vinegar
¼ cup (2 fl oz/60 ml) extra-virgin olive oil

In a small bowl stir together the garlic, honey and salt to taste until well mixed. Add the vinegar and then the oil, stirring vigorously until blended. Let stand for about 10 minutes to allow the flavors to marry.

Makes about ⅓ cup (3 fl oz/80 ml)

Herb Vinaigrette

Simple Vinaigrette

Country Dressing

MAYONNAISE BASICS

Using the speed and power of a food processor to make perfect mayonnaise every time

Making mayonnaise was once an excellent test of a cook's knowledge, skill and strength. It required a subtle, experienced touch to add oil drop by drop while beating egg yolks, ensuring that the mixture emulsified—that is, formed a smooth, thick, creamy blend—rather than broke up. It took stamina to go on whisking continuously as more oil was slowly incorporated and the mayonnaise mounted.

Today, electric food processors eliminate the uncertainty and work, blending egg and oil into a smooth, thick emulsion in a matter of seconds. Still, it makes good sense to observe the few precautions chefs have always followed when making mayonnaise. Start with all utensils and ingredients at room temperature, to promote the emulsion's formation.

And add the oil slowly, increasing the flow only when you can see that the mayonnaise is smoothly, flawlessly thickening. If you want a lighter mayonnaise, add whole eggs rather than the yolks alone. The greater volume will also help the processor blade to work more efficiently.

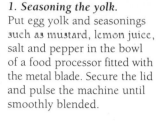

1. Seasoning the yolk.
Put egg yolk and seasonings such as mustard, lemon juice, salt and pepper in the bowl of a food processor fitted with the metal blade. Secure the lid and pulse the machine until smoothly blended.

2. Adding the oil.
With the machine running, pour the oil through the feed tube in a very thin stream. The mayonnaise will slowly begin to thicken.

3. Finishing the mayonnaise.
When about half the oil has been added and the mayonnaise is fairly thick, with the machine still running, pour in the remaining oil in a thicker stream. Continue processing until all the oil has been incorporated.

4. Adjusting the seasonings.
The finished mayonnaise should be thick enough to form soft peaks when lifted with a spatula. Taste and adjust seasonings by pulsing in a little more salt or lemon juice. To store, cover with plastic wrap, pushing the wrap directly onto the surface of the mayonnaise to prevent a skin from forming. Refrigerate for up to 3 days.

Mayonnaise

The flavor of the oil is important when making mayonnaise. Some people use a delicately flavored extra-virgin olive oil. Others combine equal parts extra-virgin olive oil and another oil. Mayonnaise is an excellent addition to salads because it is so flexible. If you need to stretch it or to make the flavor lighter, add a bit of light (single) cream. Or mix in finely chopped anchovy fillets, capers and a little garlic to create a robust mayonnaise capable of turning the simplest potato salad into a heavenly dish.

1 egg yolk
1 tablespoon fresh lemon juice
1 teaspoon Dijon mustard
salt
freshly ground pepper
⅔ cup (5 fl oz/150 ml) extra-virgin olive oil

*P*lace the egg yolk, lemon juice, mustard and salt and pepper to taste in a food processor fitted with the metal blade or in a blender; process briefly to combine. With the motor running, add the oil in a thin, steady stream and continue to blend until smooth and thickened.

Makes about ⅔ cup (6 oz/180 g)

Yogurt Dressing

The slightly tart and refreshing taste of this low-calorie dressing makes it particularly appropriate for summer salads. It can also be used as a dip for raw vegetables such as cucumber, celery, fennel, zucchini or carrot. If you like, add some minced fresh mint or dill. For a richer taste replace the parsley with 1 tablespoon paprika or with ½ teaspoon each fennel seeds, minced, and whole capers.

1 tablespoon Dijon mustard
salt
white pepper
1 tablespoon fresh lemon juice
⅔ cup (5 oz/150 g) plain yogurt
2 tablespoons extra-virgin olive oil
1 tablespoon minced fresh flat-leaf (Italian) parsley

*I*n a small bowl stir together the mustard and salt and white pepper to taste. Add the lemon juice and stir well to dissolve and blend all the ingredients. Mix in the yogurt until thoroughly incorporated, then vigorously stir in the oil. Sprinkle the parsley over the top, then mix it in well. Cover and chill for 30 minutes before serving.

Makes about 1 cup (8 fl oz/250 ml)

Yogurt Dressing

Arugula and Fig Salad

8 red figs

¼ lb (120 g) arugula (rocket), stemmed

5 tablespoons (3 fl oz/80 ml) extra-virgin olive oil

salt

cayenne pepper

6 oz (185 g) fresh goat cheese, crumbled

Use russet-colored figs, which are plump and have a thin skin. If red figs are unavailable, black or green figs will also work well. Wrapping the figs in a cloth and refrigerating them for a couple of hours makes them easier to cut.

Wrap the figs in a cloth and refrigerate for 2 hours.

Arrange the arugula on a serving platter. In a small bowl stir together the oil and salt and cayenne pepper to taste until well mixed. Cut the unpeeled figs crosswise into thin slices and arrange atop the arugula. Scatter the cheese over the figs. Stir the dressing again, pour it over the salad and serve.

Serves 4

Roasted Bell Pepper Salad

2 large yellow bell peppers
  (capsicums)
2 large red bell peppers (capsicums)
1 clove garlic
salt
freshly ground pepper
1 tablespoon minced fresh flat-leaf
  (Italian) parsley
6 tablespoons (3 fl oz/90 ml) extra-
  virgin olive oil

There is probably no more delicious way to prepare bell peppers. Once made, they can be kept in a tightly sealed container in the refrigerator for a few days, enhancing the flavor even more. If you like, increase the quantity of garlic and add some minced fresh basil. This salad is delicious served with roasted garlic heads.

Preheat an oven to 350°F (180°C).

Arrange the peppers in a shallow baking dish and bake in the oven, turning them over every so often, until they become completely soft, about 30 minutes.

Remove from the oven and, while the peppers are still warm, peel them. Split in half lengthwise and remove and discard the stems, seeds and ribs. Cut them into long, narrow strips.

Rub the inside of a shallow bowl with the garlic clove. Arrange the peppers in the bowl and season to taste with salt and pepper. Sprinkle with the parsley and drizzle with the oil. Stir well and let stand at room temperature for a couple of hours before serving to allow the flavors to marry, then serve.

Serves 4

Cucumber Salad with Dill

4 cucumbers
salt
3 cloves garlic
⅔ cup (5 oz/150 g) plain yogurt
1 tablespoon fresh lemon juice
2 tablespoons minced fresh dill
white pepper
3 tablespoons extra-virgin olive oil

A lovely summertime salad typical of the southern Mediterranean. It can be served as a side dish or an appetizer, and is also delicious tossed with herb vinaigrette (recipe on page 11) in place of the yogurt dressing. A few slices of onion are an interesting addition, and a bed of greens makes an attractive presentation.

Peel and thinly slice the cucumbers, then place the slices on a flat plate. Salt lightly and tilt the plate so that excess water will drain off easily. Let stand for about 1 hour.

Pass the garlic cloves through a garlic press into a small bowl. Add the yogurt, lemon juice, dill and salt and white pepper to taste; stir until well mixed. Add the oil and stir vigorously until blended.

Place the drained cucumber slices in a salad bowl, pour the dressing over the top and toss gently. Refrigerate for about 1 hour to allow the flavors to marry, then serve.

Serves 4

Grapefruit and Fennel Salad

2 pink grapefruits
2 fennel bulbs, thinly sliced crosswise
½ cup (3 oz/90 g) almonds, coarsely
  chopped
3 tablespoons apple juice
¼ cup (2 oz/60 g) plain yogurt
salt
freshly ground green peppercorns
1 tablespoon chopped fresh flat-leaf
  (Italian) parsley

A very light salad, perfect for those on a diet. Apples or strawberries go well alongside or in place of the grapefruit, in which case mint leaves should be used instead of parsley. Pine nuts are an elegant substitute for the almonds. Pesticide-free edible flowers make an attractive garnish.

*P*eel and section the grapefruits; carefully remove all the white membrane surrounding each segment and any seeds. Place in a salad bowl and add the fennel and almonds.

In a small bowl stir together the apple juice, yogurt and salt and ground green peppercorns to taste until well mixed. Pour the dressing over the salad and toss well. Sprinkle with the parsley and serve.

Serves 4

Vegetables with Olive Oil Dip

2 heads Belgian endive
(chicory/witloof)
2 green (spring) onions
2 carrots, peeled
4 small celery stalks
1 yellow bell pepper (capsicum),
seeded, deribbed and cut into long,
thin strips
4 radishes
1¼ cups (10 fl oz/300 ml) extra-virgin
olive oil
1 teaspoon salt
freshly ground pepper

More than anything, this dish, called pinzimonio *in Italian, is a way to enjoy seasonal vegetables. Your choice of vegetables is unlimited, although those with a crunchy texture are best because they are simpler to hold and dip into the dressing. The extra-virgin olive oil must be one of exceptional flavor; if you like, add herbs to the oil, such as a teaspoon of minced oregano or some minced garlic. Or replace the olive oil dip with the herb vinaigrette on page 11. This dish is served at the table with the dressing in a single bowl into which everyone dips their vegetables.*

Cut the endives, onions, carrots and celery stalks in half lengthwise.

Arrange all the vegetables on a large serving dish, leaving a space at the center for the bowl of dressing.

In a small bowl stir together the oil, salt and pepper to taste. Place the bowl in the center of the dish and serve.

Serves 4

Orange and Onion Salad

4 oranges
1 red (Spanish) onion, cut into paper-
    thin slices
1 teaspoon fresh oregano leaves
pinch of salt
freshly ground pepper
¼ cup (2 fl oz/60 ml) extra-virgin
    olive oil
black olives for garnish

Here is a popular Sicilian salad that makes an excellent appetizer or a side dish with chicken, duck, turkey or any wild fowl. If you want to give the raw onion a milder taste, soak it in cold water to cover for 30 minutes, then drain and dry before combining it with the oranges.

Peel the oranges, carefully removing all the white membrane. Cut crosswise into thin slices and remove any seeds. Arrange the slices on a large serving dish. Place the onion slices on top. Scatter the oregano over the onions. Sprinkle with the salt and pepper to taste and then drizzle with the oil. Garnish with black olives. Refrigerate until ready to serve.

Serves 4

Apple and Chicory Salad

1 tablespoon fresh lemon juice
3 red apples
3 celery stalks, thinly sliced crosswise
1 small heart of chicory (curly endive),
    torn into pieces
⅔ cup (5 fl oz/150 ml) sour cream
2 tablespoons plain yogurt
1 tablespoon freshly grated
    horseradish
salt
freshly ground pepper
6 walnut halves, coarsely chopped

Quick and easy to prepare, this perfect summer salad can be enriched with Swiss cheese, cut into cubes, and tossed with mayonnaise (recipe on page 13) in place of the sour cream dressing. Another pleasant addition is a thick slice of ham, cut into small pieces.

*F*ill a large bowl with water and add the lemon juice. Core the apples, but do not peel them. Cut them into 1-inch (2.5-cm) chunks, dropping them into the bowl of water as they are cut. Drain well and add to a salad bowl along with the celery and chicory.

In a small bowl stir together the sour cream, yogurt, horseradish and salt and pepper to taste until well mixed. Pour the dressing over the salad, add the walnuts, toss and serve.

Serves 4

Tomato and Pepper Mold

10 oz (300 g) fresh tomatoes, peeled,
    or 1 cup (8 fl oz/250 ml) tomato
    juice
2 cups (16 fl oz/500 ml) chicken stock
4 teaspoons unflavored gelatin
pinch of cayenne pepper
1 tablespoon minced fresh thyme
1 teaspoon sugar
salt
1 red bell pepper (capsicum), about
    3 oz (90 g), seeded, deribbed and
    cut into thin strips
1 yellow bell pepper (capsicum),
    about 3 oz (90 g), seeded, deribbed
    and cut into thin strips

With its sophisticated coloring, this brilliant red molded salad is an excellent appetizer prepared in individual molds for a formal lunch, or in a large mold for a buffet meal. The amount of cayenne pepper can be adjusted, or even eliminated, according to personal taste.

*I*f using fresh tomatoes, pass them through a coarse sieve and then through a fine-mesh sieve to produce a thin sauce. You should have about 1 cup (8 fl oz/250 ml). Set aside.

Pour 1 cup (8 fl oz/250 ml) of the stock into a small saucepan and add the gelatin. Let stand to soften for 3 minutes. Place the pan over low heat and stir until the gelatin dissolves. Remove from the heat and pour into a bowl. Add the remaining 1 cup (8 fl oz/250 ml) stock and stir well. Stir in the sieved tomatoes or tomato juice, cayenne pepper, thyme, sugar and salt to taste. Let stand until the gelatin begins to set, about 30 minutes.

Mix in the bell peppers. Rinse a 1-qt (32-fl oz/1-l) mold in cold water. Pour in the stock mixture, cover and chill for a few hours until set.

Carefully run a knife tip around the edge of the mold. Dip the mold briefly in hot water, invert a serving plate on top and invert the mold. Serve at once.

Serves 4

Artichoke and Fennel Salad

2 tablespoons fresh lemon juice
4 young, tender artichokes, about 5 oz
   (150 g) each
2 fennel bulbs, thinly sliced crosswise
1 tablespoon minced fresh dill
1 handful of minced fresh mint
salt
white pepper
¼ cup (2 fl oz/60 ml) extra-virgin
   olive oil

Use only the most tender part of the artichoke—the heart and pale leaves that surround it. For a richer salad use yogurt dressing (recipe on page 13) in place of the oil. To make a more ample salad, thinly slice an uncooked beef fillet (about ¾ lb/375 g), dress the slices with balsamic vinegar and add them to the bowl with the vegetables.

*F*ill a large bowl with water and add 1 tablespoon of the lemon juice. Trim off the stem and remove the outer leaves from each artichoke until you reach the pale, tender inner leaves. As each artichoke is stripped, cut it in half lengthwise, trim away any thorny choke, and drop the halves into the water. Drain, pat dry with paper towels and cut lengthwise into thin slices. Place the slices in a salad bowl, add the remaining 1 tablespoon lemon juice and toss to prevent discoloration.

   Arrange the fennel slices in the bowl with the artichokes. Sprinkle with the dill and mint and then with salt and white pepper to taste. Drizzle with the oil and serve immediately.

Serves 4

Tomatoes Stuffed with Eggs and Anchovies

4 tomatoes
1 teaspoon Dijon mustard
salt
¼ cup (2 fl oz/60 ml) extra-virgin
olive oil
1 teaspoon minced fresh flat-leaf
(Italian) parsley
1 teaspoon minced fresh mint
1 teaspoon minced fresh basil
4 anchovy fillets in oil, drained and
cut into small pieces
3 eggs, hard-cooked and cut into
cubes
4 thin slices lemon
12 well-drained capers
4 leaves curly-leaf parsley

Ideal for hot-weather dining, these stuffed tomatoes can also be served chilled. For an even simpler dish, fill each tomato with a generous spoonful of mayonnaise (recipe on page 13). Serve as a side dish with cold fish or meat, or as a first course. Stuffed tomatoes make a wonderful addition to a buffet table; simply triple or quadruple the recipe as needed.

❊

Slice the top off of each tomato. Using a spoon, gently remove the pulp and seeds. Lightly salt the insides and then invert onto a plate for 30 minutes to drain.

In a small bowl stir together the mustard and salt to taste until well mixed. Add the oil and stir vigorously until blended. Add the flat-leaf parsley, mint, basil, anchovies and eggs; mix well.

Turn the tomatoes cut side up and place on a serving dish. Fill each tomato with one-fourth of the mixture. Place 1 lemon slice atop each tomato. Decorate each slice with 3 capers and a parsley leaf and serve.

Serves 4

Spinach and Apple Salad with Bacon

2 apples
a few drops of fresh lemon juice
¼ lb (120 g) sliced bacon
1 tablespoon Dijon mustard
1–2 tablespoons balsamic vinegar
salt
white pepper
¼ cup (2 fl oz/60 ml) extra-virgin
   olive oil
½ lb (250 g) spinach, stemmed and
   washed
12 black olives, pitted and chopped
2 eggs, hard-cooked and cut into
   wedges, for garnish

Choose young spinach leaves for this salad. If only more mature leaves are available, tenderize them by sprinkling with lemon juice and allowing them to "marinate" for a few minutes.

Peel the apples, if desired, then core and chop. Place in a bowl, sprinkle with the lemon juice and toss lightly; set aside.

In a frying pan over high heat, fry the bacon until crisp, about 5 minutes. Transfer to paper towels to drain. Cut into small pieces; set aside.

In a small bowl stir together the mustard and vinegar, salt and white pepper to taste until well mixed. Add the oil and stir vigorously until blended. Set aside for a few minutes to allow the flavors to blend.

Place the spinach leaves in a salad bowl. Add the apples, bacon, olives and dressing and toss well. Garnish with the egg wedges and serve.

Serves 4

Bruschetta

4 thick slices coarse country bread
2 cloves garlic
2 tomatoes
salt
freshly ground pepper
4 tablespoons (2 fl oz/60 ml) extra-
    virgin olive oil
4 fresh basil leaves

This Roman specialty reverses the customary roles of salad ingredients: the usually modest crouton becomes the leading player, while the vegetables and other toppings are the supporting cast. There are many other possible additions— small leaves of arugula (rocket) or watercress, shavings of Parmesan, drops of balsamic vinegar, anchovy fillets, capers, fresh oregano leaves. Or place a spoonful of mayonnaise (recipe on page 13) on top of the tomatoes and omit the oil.

Toast the bread slices in a toaster until the outsides are crunchy but the insides are still soft.

Cut the garlic cloves in half lengthwise. Using a half clove for each bread slice, evenly and thoroughly rub one side of the toast with the cut side of the garlic. Cut each tomato into 6–8 wedges and divide the wedges evenly among the bread slices, arranging them on the garlic-rubbed sides. Sprinkle each toast with salt and pepper to taste and then drizzle with 1 tablespoon of the oil. Finally, garnish each toast with a basil leaf and serve.

Serves 4

Grape and Carrot Mold

2 cups (16 fl oz/500 ml) chicken stock
4 teaspoons unflavored gelatin
¼ cup (2 fl oz/60 ml) fresh lemon
  juice
1 tablespoon Worcestershire sauce
2 tablespoons finely chopped fresh
  flat-leaf (Italian) parsley
salt
white pepper
1 bunch seedless green grapes, about
  10 oz (300 g), stemmed and cut in
  half
4 carrots, about 6 oz (185 g) total
  weight, peeled and cut lengthwise
  into thin strips

*Very refined, this exquisite molded salad can be served as
an appetizer for an elegant meal, perhaps prepared in
individual molds, or between courses to freshen the palate. It
is also a suitable accompaniment to meat and cheese dishes.*

*P*our 1 cup (8 fl oz/250 ml) of the stock into a small
saucepan and add the gelatin. Let stand to soften for 3
minutes. Place the pan over low heat and stir until the
gelatin dissolves. Remove from the heat and pour into a
bowl. Add the remaining 1 cup (8 fl oz/250 ml) stock,
the lemon juice, Worcestershire sauce, parsley and salt
and white pepper to taste; stir well.

Rinse a 1-qt (32-fl oz/1-l) mold (or small individual
molds) in cold water and pour in enough of the stock
mixture to form a thin layer. Let stand for 30 minutes.

Add the grapes and carrots to the mold and then pour
in the remaining stock mixture. Cover and chill for a few
hours until set.

Carefully run a knife tip around the edge of the mold.
Dip the mold briefly in hot water, invert a serving plate
on top and invert the mold. Serve at once.

Serves 4

Tomatoes and Mozzarella

1 bunch of fresh basil leaves

4 tomatoes, thinly sliced

¾ lb (400 g) fresh mozzarella cheese, thinly sliced

1 tablespoon capers

8 black olives

4 anchovy fillets in oil, drained and cut into small pieces

salt

¼ cup (2 fl oz/60 ml) extra-virgin olive oil

A classic combination of Neapolitan cuisine. Quick to prepare, this salad is extremely delicious, but only if you use top-quality ingredients: vine-ripened tomatoes and the freshest mozzarella. If you like, use oregano or thyme in place of the basil. Pickled cucumbers or baby onions, used in moderation, also work well with this salad.

Set aside the prettiest basil leaves for garnish.

Arrange the tomato and mozzarella slices and the remaining basil leaves on a serving dish, alternating the slices and the leaves. If you have any leftover tomato slices, arrange them in an attractive pattern in the center of the dish.

Rinse the capers under cold running water, drain and pat dry with paper towels.

Decorate the plate with the capers, olives and anchovy pieces. Scatter the reserved basil leaves on top, tearing any large leaves. Sprinkle to taste with salt, drizzle the oil in a thin stream over the top and serve.

Serves 4

Shrimp and Asparagus Salad

1 lb (500 g) shrimp (prawns) in
  the shell
24 slender asparagus
1 egg yolk
cayenne pepper
salt
⅓ cup (3 fl oz/90 ml) extra-virgin
  olive oil
⅓ cup (3 fl oz/90 ml) sesame oil,
  preferably cold-pressed
1 tablespoon fresh lemon juice
8 leaves green leaf lettuce

*Arrange this elegant and decorative salad on a large platter
to show it off best. Choose the prettiest lettuce leaves, all more
or less of the same size, for the most stunning presentation. If
it is difficult to find asparagus, you can substitute avocado,
sliced and moistened with a little lemon juice.*

*F*ill a saucepan with salted water and bring to a boil.
Boil the shrimp until they turn pink and curl slightly,
2–3 minutes. Drain, place under cold running water and
drain again. Peel and devein the shrimp and set aside.

Bind the asparagus together into a bundle with kitchen
string. Fill a tall, narrow saucepan halfway with water
and stand the asparagus in it, with the tips above the
waterline. Bring to a boil and boil until just tender when
pierced with a knife, about 8 minutes. Remove from the
pan and discard the string; let cool. Cut off the top 2
inches (5 cm) and reserve; save the stems for another use.

Put the egg yolk and cayenne pepper and salt to taste
in a blender or in a food processor fitted with the metal
blade; process briefly to combine. With the motor
running, add the olive oil and sesame oil in a thin
stream. When the mixture thickens to a mayonnaise
consistency, transfer to a bowl and stir in the lemon
juice. Reserve some of the nicest-looking shrimp for a
garnish; mix the remaining shrimp into the mayonnaise.

Arrange the lettuce leaves on a large platter and spoon
the shrimp mixture on top. Decorate with the reserved
asparagus tips and shrimp. Serve at once.

Serves 4

Smoked Chicken Salad with Grapes

1 small bunch seedless green or red grapes, about ¼ lb (125 g), stemmed and cut in half

1 yellow bell pepper (capsicum), seeded, deribbed and chopped

3 celery stalks, chopped

1 lb (500 g) boned smoked chicken, cut into small cubes

1 heart of butter lettuce, separated into leaves

2 tablespoons fresh orange juice

1 tablespoon tarragon vinegar

salt

white pepper

¼ cup (2 fl oz/60 ml) sunflower seed oil, preferably cold-pressed

1 tablespoon minced fresh tarragon

Satisfy your taste whims with different fruits in this pleasant salad. For example, substitute small pieces of melon, fig or mango for the grapes. You can also use poached or roasted chicken in place of the smoked chicken, in which case yogurt dressing (recipe on page 13) should stand in for the sunflower oil dressing.

*P*lace the grapes, bell pepper, celery and chicken in a salad bowl. Add the lettuce, tearing any large leaves in half. Set aside.

In a small bowl stir together the orange juice, vinegar and salt and white pepper to taste until well mixed. Add the oil and tarragon and stir vigorously until blended. Pour the dressing over the salad, toss gently and serve.

Serves 4

Beef Fillet and Parmesan Salad

¾ lb (375 g) beef fillet

¼ cup (2 fl oz/60 ml) balsamic vinegar

salt

6 tablespoons (3 fl oz/90 ml) extra-
   virgin olive oil

1 head radicchio (red chicory), torn
   into pieces

2 oz (60 g) Parmesan cheese

Here is a popular Italian raw beef salad that is both light and flavorful. Watercress can be used in place of the radicchio. Another version marinates the beef in balsamic vinegar for an hour, and then grills it before slicing and adding to the salad.

Place the beef fillet in a freezer for about 20 minutes. (This makes it slightly firm and easier to slice.)

Meanwhile, in a shallow bowl stir together the vinegar and salt to taste until well mixed. Add the oil and stir vigorously until blended.

Make a bed of the radicchio on a large serving platter. Slice the beef fillet on the diagonal into slices so thin as to be almost transparent. Dip each slice into the oil mixture and then lay the slices on the radicchio. Using a sharp knife or a vegetable peeler, cut the Parmesan into paper-thin shavings. Scatter them evenly over the meat and serve.

Serves 4

Pasta and Salmon Salad

¾ lb (360 g) shrimp (prawns) in
   the shell
3 tablespoons curry powder
½ lb (240 g) short pasta
¼ lb (120 g) smoked salmon, thinly
   sliced and cut into long, narrow
   strips
1½ cups (12 oz/375 g) well-drained
   cooked or canned chick-peas
   (garbanzo beans)
1 tablespoon minced fresh tarragon
1 teaspoon fresh lemon juice
salt
freshly ground pepper
3 tablespoons extra-virgin olive oil

*A delicate harmony of colors distinguishes this attractive cold
salad. The pasta is boiled with curry powder, which imparts
an intense yellow hue that contrasts beautifully with the pink
of the salmon. The pasta should be very firm to the bite or the
salad will not have the proper texture. Farfalle (bowties) or
conchiglie (shells) would be a good choice for the pasta.*

*F*ill a saucepan with salted water and bring to a boil.
Boil the shrimp until they turn pink and curl slightly,
2–3 minutes. Drain, place under cold running water and
drain again. Peel and devein the shrimp and set aside.

  Fill a large saucepan with salted water and bring to a
boil. Add the curry powder, let it dissolve, then add the
pasta. When the pasta is cooked but still firm, drain and
cool under cold running water. Drain again thoroughly
and place in a salad bowl. Add the shrimp, salmon and
chick-peas.

  In a small bowl stir together the tarragon, lemon juice
and salt and pepper to taste until well mixed. Add the oil
and stir vigorously until blended. Pour the dressing over
the salad, toss well and serve.

Serves 4

Sliced Beef and Potato Salad

2 boiling potatoes, about ¾ lb (375 g)
  total weight
10 oz (300 g) boiled beef, at room
  temperature
2 tablespoons balsamic vinegar
salt
freshly ground pepper
2 tablespoons extra-virgin olive oil
1 white onion, sliced paper-thin
2 dill pickles (pickled cucumbers),
  thinly sliced
2 tomatoes, thinly sliced

This tasty salad is usually made with leftover cooked beef. It is equally delicious prepared with roast beef instead of boiled beef. If you are making the salad from scratch, put 1 pound (500 g) boiling beef in a heavy pot with salted water to cover. Add onions and carrots and cook gently until very tender, about 2 hours. Mayonnaise (recipe on page 13) is another excellent topping for this salad.

Put the potatoes in a saucepan, add salted water to cover and bring to a boil. Cook over medium heat until tender when pierced with a fork, 15–20 minutes. Drain and peel while still hot. Let cool, then cut crosswise into thin slices. Set aside.

Remove any fat and gristle from the beef and slice it thinly.

In a small bowl stir together the balsamic vinegar and salt and pepper to taste until well mixed. Add the oil and stir vigorously until blended.

In a large, shallow salad bowl, arrange the beef, potato, onion, pickle and tomato slices. Stir the dressing once again and slowly pour it over the slices. Serve at once.

Serves 4

Caesar Salad

⅓ cup (3 fl oz/90 ml) extra-virgin olive oil

4 cloves garlic, sliced lengthwise

4 thick slices coarse country bread, crusts removed and bread cut into ¾-inch (2-cm) cubes

1 head romaine (cos) lettuce, separated into leaves

4 anchovy fillets in olive oil, drained

2 tablespoons capers

1 egg

1 tablespoon fresh lemon juice

1 tablespoon Worcestershire sauce

1 teaspoon coarse-grain mustard

1½ oz (50 g) Parmesan cheese, cut into shavings

Capers give this famous salad an Italian accent. If possible, steep the garlic cloves in the olive oil for at least an hour before using them.

In a frying pan over high heat, combine the oil and garlic and fry the garlic until brown, about 4 minutes. Remove the garlic and discard. Add the bread cubes to the pan and fry over high heat, stirring often, until browned. Transfer to paper towels to drain.

Tear the large and medium-sized lettuce leaves coarsely and leave the small leaves whole. Put the lettuce in a large salad bowl. In a smaller bowl mash the anchovies with a fork. Rinse the capers under cold running water, drain and pat dry with paper towels. Add to the anchovies along with the bread cubes and toss to mix.

Bring a small saucepan filled with water to a boil, gently slip in the egg, remove from the heat and let stand for 1 minute. Remove the egg from the pan, immerse it in cold water and break it into a small bowl. Add the lemon juice, Worcestershire sauce and mustard and stir vigorously until well blended. Add the anchovy mixture to the lettuce. Pour the dressing over the salad, scatter the Parmesan over the top, toss delicately and serve.

Serves 4

Turkey and Belgian Endive Salad

4 small heads Belgian endive
  (chicory/witloof)
1 lb (500 g) cooked turkey breast,
  thinly sliced
½ cup (2 oz/50 g) walnuts or
  hazelnuts (filberts), plus a few for
  garnish
¼ cup (2 fl oz/60 ml) extra-virgin
  olive oil
¼ cup (2 fl oz/60 ml) fresh lemon
  juice
salt

Other types of young salad greens can be substituted for the Belgian endive, as long as the leaves are small and the greens are in season. For a more substantial salad, add 2 oz (60 g) Roquefort cheese, cut into very small pieces, and substitute a more neutrally flavored seed oil, such as sunflower, for the extra-virgin olive oil.

Tear the endive leaves coarsely and arrange them in a serving dish. Lay the turkey slices on the leaves.

In the work bowl of a food processor fitted with the metal blade, combine the nuts, oil, lemon juice and salt to taste. Process until a smooth cream forms. Spoon the dressing over the salad, garnish with the extra nuts and serve.

Serves 4

Bean and Shrimp Salad

1¼ cups (8 oz/250 g) dried small
   white (navy) beans or borlotti beans
salt
½ white onion or 2 green (spring)
   onions, cut into paper-thin slices
juice of ½ lemon
freshly ground green peppercorns
5 tablespoons (3 fl oz/80 ml) extra-
   virgin olive oil
½ lb (250 g) shrimp (prawns) in
   the shell
1 tablespoon minced fresh flat-leaf
   (Italian) parsley
1 small head Bibb lettuce, about 5 oz
   (150 g), separated into leaves

A classic variation on this recipe, tasty but certainly less refined, substitutes a mixture of cut-up anchovy fillets, minced garlic and parsley for the shrimp.

Place the beans in a bowl, add water to cover by ½ inch (12 mm) and let stand overnight. The next day, drain the beans and put them in a saucepan. Add water to cover by 1 inch (2.5 cm) and salt lightly. Bring to a boil, reduce the heat to low and simmer, partially covered, until tender, about 1½ hours. Drain well and let cool.

Meanwhile, arrange the onion slices in a salad bowl. In a small bowl stir together the lemon juice and salt and ground green peppercorns to taste until well mixed. Add the oil and stir vigorously until well blended. Pour over the onions, toss gently and let stand for a few hours.

Bring a saucepan filled with water to a boil, add the shrimp and boil until they turn pink and curl slightly, 2–3 minutes. Drain, place under cold running water and drain again. Peel and devein the shrimp and add to the bowl. Add the beans and parsley and toss gently.

Place the lettuce leaves on a serving platter. Spoon the shrimp mixture over the top and serve.

Serves 4

Niçoise Salad

2 boiling potatoes, about ¾ lb (375 g) total weight

½ lb (250 g) green beans, trimmed

2 tablespoons capers

4 tomatoes, about ¾ lb (375 g) total weight, cut into 6–8 wedges

1 can (7 oz/210 g) tuna in olive oil, drained and flaked

1 tablespoon minced fresh oregano

1 tablespoon Dijon mustard

2 tablespoons white wine vinegar

salt

5 tablespoons (3 fl oz/80 ml) extra-virgin olive oil

¼ lb (120 g) black olives for garnish

A classic Provençal salad with the true flavor of the sea. Toss the salad or, to show off its striking colors, arrange the ingredients on individual plates. Herb vinaigrette (recipe on page 11) can be used in place of the dressing.

Put the potatoes in a saucepan, add salted water to cover and bring to a boil. Cook over medium heat until tender when pierced with a fork, 15–20 minutes. Drain and peel while still hot. Let cool, then cut into 1-inch (2.5-cm) cubes. Place in a salad bowl.

Meanwhile, fill another saucepan with salted water and bring to a boil. Add the green beans and boil just until tender, about 5 minutes. Drain, place under cold running water and drain again. Add to the potatoes.

Rinse the capers under cold running water, drain and pat dry with paper towels. Add to the salad bowl along with the tomatoes and tuna. Sprinkle the oregano over the top.

In a small bowl stir together the mustard, vinegar and salt to taste until well blended. Vigorously stir in the olive oil until well mixed. Pour the dressing over the salad and toss well. Garnish with the olives and serve.

Serves 4

Pasta Salad with Tomato and Bell Pepper

2 tablespoons capers

3 tomatoes, peeled and finely chopped

1 yellow bell pepper (capsicum), seeded, deribbed and finely chopped

3 celery stalks, thinly sliced

8 fresh basil leaves, shredded

1 teaspoon fresh lemon juice

salt

5 tablespoons (3 fl oz/80 ml) extra-virgin olive oil

½ lb (250 g) fusilli

This typical pasta salad lends itself to many other types of pasta, such as conchiglie (shells) or rigatoni (tubes). The only rule is that the pasta must be short and wide. Fresh oregano is a pleasant alternative to the basil. For a more filling salad, add mozzarella cheese, cut into small cubes.

Rinse the capers under cold running water and pat dry with paper towels. Place in a large salad bowl with the tomatoes, bell pepper, celery and basil.

In a small bowl stir together the lemon juice and salt to taste until well mixed. Add the oil and stir vigorously until blended.

Meanwhile, fill a large saucepan with salted water and bring to a boil. Add the pasta and boil until cooked but still firm. Drain and then cool under cold running water. Drain again thoroughly and add to the salad bowl. Pour the dressing over the salad, toss well and serve.

Serves 4

Asian Chicken Salad

¼ red (Spanish) onion, thinly sliced

2 cloves garlic, minced

2 teaspoons grated fresh ginger

1 teaspoon sugar

2 tablespoons white rice vinegar

3 tablespoons peanut oil

1 teaspoon chili oil

2 tablespoons soy sauce

pinch of salt, optional

3 chicken breast halves

1 cucumber, peeled, seeded and cut
into matchsticks

1 red bell pepper (capsicum), seeded,
deribbed and cut into matchsticks

1 cup (3 oz/90 g) bean sprouts

2 cups (6 oz/180 g) coarsely chopped
red cabbage

2 tablespoons chopped fresh cilantro
(fresh coriander)

½ cup (2 oz/60 g) chopped roasted
peanuts

The secret to preparing this light and simple salad is hand cutting the ingredients into matchstick-sized strips to achieve a uniform texture. Chinese (nappa) cabbage can be successfully substituted for the red cabbage. Crisp crackers are a good accompaniment.

*I*n a small bowl combine the onion, garlic, ginger and sugar. Stir in the vinegar, peanut oil, chili oil and soy sauce until well mixed. Season with salt, if desired. Let stand while you prepare the remaining ingredients.

Fill a saucepan with salted water and bring to a boil. Add the chicken breasts, reduce the heat and simmer for 10 minutes. Skim off any foam on the surface, turn off the heat, cover the pan and let stand for 15 minutes.

Drain the chicken breasts and let cool completely, then bone and skin them. Cut the chicken meat into long, thin strips and place in a salad bowl. Add the cucumber, bell pepper, bean sprouts and cabbage. Pour the dressing over the salad and toss well. Sprinkle with the cilantro and peanuts and serve.

Serves 4

Ham and Celery Salad with Walnuts

1 bunch celery, about 1¼ lb (600 g)
1 head romaine (cos) lettuce,
  shredded
2 slices cooked ham, about 3 oz (90 g)
  each, cut into long, thin strips
juice of ½ lemon
salt
5 tablespoons (3 fl oz/80 ml) extra-
  virgin olive oil
½ cup (2 oz/60 g) walnuts, chopped

To make this light, fresh salad more substantial, add sliced fresh mushrooms and Swiss cheese.

Select only the palest, most tender stalks of the celery bunch; reserve the remaining stalks for another use. Cut the stalks crosswise into thin slices and place in a salad bowl. Add the lettuce and ham and toss together.

In a small bowl stir together the lemon juice and salt to taste until well mixed. Add the oil and stir vigorously until blended. Pour the dressing over the salad and toss well. Scatter the walnuts over the top and serve.

Serves 4

New Potato Salad

1½ lb (800 g) red new potatoes
1 cup (8 fl oz/250 ml) dry white wine
2 tablespoons minced fresh flat-leaf
  (Italian) parsley
1 clove garlic, minced
1 tablespoon white wine vinegar
salt
½ cup (4 fl oz/125 ml) extra-virgin
  olive oil

This salad is an excellent accompaniment to meat dishes, such as grilled sausages. For a slightly tart flavor, add finely chopped sorrel instead of parsley to the dressing. Or you can use mayonnaise (recipe on page 13) in place of the wine dressing. When making the mayonnaise, add 1 small can (3½ oz/100 g) tuna in olive oil, well drained, once the mayonnaise is thick, and process until well mixed.

Put the potatoes in a saucepan, add salted water to cover and bring to a boil. Cook over medium heat until tender when pierced with a fork, 15–20 minutes. Drain and peel, if desired, while still hot. Cut the potatoes into large pieces and place in a salad bowl. Immediately pour the wine over the potatoes and sprinkle with the parsley and garlic.

In a small bowl stir together the vinegar and salt to taste until well mixed. Add the oil and stir vigorously until blended. Pour the dressing over the potatoes and mix gently, being careful not to break up the potatoes. Serve at once. If the salad is to be served cold, let the potatoes cool before dressing them.

Serves 4

Mixed Green Salad

country dressing *(recipe on page 11)*

1 large handful of green leaf lettuce leaves, about 3 oz (90 g), torn if large

1 large handful of romaine (cos) lettuce leaves, about 3 oz (90 g), torn if large

1 small bunch arugula (rocket), stemmed

1 cucumber, peeled and thinly sliced

1 green bell pepper (capsicum), seeded, deribbed and finely chopped

All kinds of greens work with this salad: butter or Bibb lettuce, escarole, oakleaf lettuce, tender spinach leaves, dandelion, watercress and radicchio (red chicory). If you prefer, substitute yogurt dressing (recipe on page 13) for the country dressing.

*P*repare the country dressing and set aside to allow the flavors to marry.

Arrange the lettuces and arugula in a salad bowl. Add the cucumber and bell pepper. Pour the dressing over the salad, toss and serve.

Serves 4

Lemon and Fennel Salad

1 lemon
3 fennel bulbs, thinly sliced crosswise
2 tablespoons cumin seeds
salt
freshly ground green peppercorns
¼ cup (2 fl oz/60 ml) extra-virgin
  olive oil

Serve this refreshing salad alongside baked or grilled fish. The cumin seeds may be replaced by fresh dill, poppyseeds or, for a slightly spicier flavor, mustard seeds.

*P*eel the lemon, carefully removing all the white membrane. Cut crosswise into very thin slices and remove any seeds.

  Combine the fennel and lemon slices in a salad bowl. Add the cumin seeds and salt and ground green peppercorns to taste; mix well. Drizzle the oil over the top and toss again. Let stand for 10 minutes to allow the flavors to blend, then serve.

Serves 4

Cabbage Salad with Cumin Seeds

1 head Savoy cabbage, about 13 oz
  (400 g)
½ cup (4 fl oz/125 ml) heavy
  whipping (double) cream
1 tablespoon red wine vinegar
1 tablespoon sugar
salt
white pepper
1 tablespoon cumin seeds

Raw cabbage—either green or white—makes an excellent salad. A chopped apple and 2 tablespoons raisins are possible additions. An alternative dressing can be made using extra-virgin olive oil, pressed garlic, anchovy paste and vinegar.

Remove and discard the larger leaves from the cabbage, then cut it lengthwise into quarters. Cut each quarter into long, very thin strips. Set aside.

  In a salad bowl stir together the cream, vinegar, sugar and salt and white pepper to taste. Add the cabbage and mix gently. Sprinkle with the cumin seeds and let stand for 30 minutes before serving to allow the flavors to blend.

Serves 4

Watercress and Orange Salad

1¼ lb (600 g) watercress
2 oranges
4 celery stalks, thinly sliced crosswise
1 tablespoon fresh lemon juice
1 tablespoon white wine vinegar
1 tablespoon curry powder
salt
freshly ground pepper
5 tablespoons (3 fl oz/80 ml) extra-
   virgin olive oil

A salad with sunny Mediterranean flavors that is a fine accompaniment to fish or lamb. Use only pale, very tender celery stalks and the small, tender leaves of the watercress sprigs. Avocado slices can be used in place of the orange slices or, for a more substantial dish, add smoked herring fillet and a few olives.

Remove and discard the tough stems and leaves from the watercress. Arrange in a salad bowl. Peel the oranges, being sure to eliminate all the white membrane, then slice them crosswise and remove any seeds. Add to the bowl, along with the celery.

In a small bowl stir together the lemon juice, vinegar, curry powder and salt and pepper to taste until well mixed. Add the oil and stir vigorously until blended. Pour the dressing over the salad, toss well and serve.

Serves 4

Broccoli and Avocado Salad

1½ lb (800 g) young, tender broccoli
1 avocado
2 tablespoons fresh lemon juice
½ cup (2 oz/60 g) pecans, coarsely
   chopped
1 tablespoon Dijon mustard
salt
¼ cup (2 fl oz/60 ml) extra-virgin
   olive oil
1 tablespoon minced fresh flat-leaf
   (Italian) parsley

Nutritious and flavorful, this salad pairs well with pork, poultry or game. To serve as a main dish, add crab or lobster meat.

Cut the broccoli florets from the large stems. (Reserve the large stems for making soup or another use.) Fill a saucepan with salted water and bring to a boil. Add the florets and boil until barely tender, about 3 minutes. Drain, cool under cold running water and drain again. Set aside.

   Peel and pit the avocado and cut it into cubes. Place in a small bowl and toss with 1 tablespoon of the lemon juice to prevent darkening. Place the avocado and broccoli in a salad bowl and add the nuts.

   In a small bowl stir together the remaining 1 tablespoon lemon juice, the mustard and salt to taste until well mixed. Add the oil and parsley and stir vigorously until blended. Pour the dressing over the salad, toss gently and serve.

Serves 4

Warm Potato and Chicory Salad

2 white onions, about 6 oz (200 g) total weight, unpeeled
2 russet potatoes, about 10 oz (300 g) total weight
1 heart of chicory (curly endive), torn into pieces
1 tablespoon minced fresh oregano
1 tablespoon white wine vinegar
salt
freshly ground pepper
3 tablespoons extra-virgin olive oil

The pleasure of this salad is the combination of hot and cold. It makes an excellent accompaniment to grilled or roast meats and fish. To serve it as a main course, add some flaked tuna and capers.

*P*reheat an oven to 350°F (180°C).

Place the onions in a small, shallow baking dish and bake until they are completely soft, about 1 hour.

When the onions have been cooking for 30 minutes, begin to prepare the potatoes. Peel them and cut into 1-inch (2.5-cm) cubes. Arrange on a rack above boiling water, cover and steam until tender, about 20 minutes.

Place the chicory in a salad bowl. As soon as the onions are cooked, remove and discard the skins, chop the onions coarsely and add them while still hot to the chicory. Then add the warm potatoes and sprinkle with the oregano.

In a small bowl stir together the vinegar and salt and pepper to taste until well mixed. Add the oil and stir vigorously until blended. Pour the dressing over the salad, toss well and serve immediately.

Serves 4

Broccoli and Anchovy Salad

2 lb (900 g) broccoli

2 tablespoons capers

4 anchovy fillets in oil, drained and
   cut into small pieces

⅓ cup (2 oz/60 g) black olives, pitted

⅓ cup (2 oz/60 g) green olives, pitted

1 bell pepper (capsicum), seeded,
   deribbed and cut into long, thin
   strips

2 tablespoons onion-flavored vinegar
   (*see note*)

salt

freshly ground pepper

5 tablespoons (3 fl oz/80 ml) extra-
   virgin olive oil

*An exquisite broccoli salad with the flavor of the sea. To
make onion-flavored vinegar, soak onion slices in white wine
vinegar for 30 minutes. Remove the onions before using.
Mayonnaise (recipe on page 13) would also make a good
dressing for this salad.*

Cut the broccoli florets from the large stems. (Reserve
the large stems for making soup or another use.) Fill a
saucepan with salted water and bring to a boil. Add the
florets and boil until barely tender, about 3 minutes.
Drain, cool under cold running water and drain again.
Place in a salad bowl.

Rinse the capers under cold running water, drain and
pat dry with paper towels. Add to the salad bowl along
with the anchovy fillets, black and green olives and
bell pepper.

In a small bowl stir together the vinegar and salt and
pepper to taste until well mixed. Add the oil and stir
vigorously until blended. Pour the dressing over the
salad, toss well and serve immediately.

Serves 4

Carrot and Blue Cheese Salad with Cumin

2 oz (60 g) blue cheese, at room
   temperature
1 cup (8 fl oz/250 ml) light (single)
   cream
salt
2 tablespoons sesame oil
1 lb (500 g) carrots, peeled and thinly
   sliced
1 tablespoon cumin seeds

A tasty salad that goes well with simple dishes such as grilled meats or omelets. Celery makes an interesting alternative to carrots. Sesame, poppy or mustard seeds can replace the cumin seeds. Yogurt dressing (recipe on page 13) also works well here.

In a blender or a food processor fitted with the metal blade, combine the cheese, cream and salt to taste; blend until mixed. With the motor running, add the oil in a thin, steady stream and continue to blend until the mixture is creamy.

   Arrange the carrots in a bowl, pour the dressing over the top, sprinkle with the cumin seeds and serve.

Serves 4

Pineapple Salad with Radicchio and Sprouts

1 head radicchio (red chicory),
    separated into leaves
8 slices pineapple, cut into small cubes
1 handful of pine nuts
1 teaspoon fresh lemon juice
1 tablespoon balsamic vinegar
½ teaspoon sugar
salt
freshly ground pepper
¼ cup (2 fl oz/60 ml) extra-virgin
    olive oil
¼ lb (120 g) sprouts (see note)

Use alfalfa, sunflower, mung bean or soybean sprouts for this delicate, light and healthful salad. Green leaf lettuce can replace the radicchio. To make the salad richer, add some chopped ham. The pineapple may be from a can, but it must be well drained.

Line a salad bowl with the radicchio leaves. In another bowl mix together the pineapple and pine nuts. In a small bowl stir together the lemon juice, vinegar, sugar and salt and pepper to taste until well mixed. Add the oil and stir vigorously until blended.

Pour half of the dressing over the pineapple mixture and mix well. Toss the sprouts with the remaining dressing. Spoon the pineapple mixture atop the radicchio. Garnish with the sprouts and serve.

Serves 4

Orange and Belgian Endive Salad

4 heads Belgian endive
   (chicory/witloof)
3 oranges
⅓ cup (2 oz/60 g) almonds, coarsely
   chopped
1 tablespoon fresh lemon juice
2 tablespoons fresh orange juice
¼ cup (2 fl oz/60 ml) light (single)
   cream
salt
cayenne pepper

Elegant, delicate and bittersweet, here is a salad suited to richer meats, such as salami or roast pork. To turn it into a main dish, add tuna or smoked herring, trout or salmon and paper-thin slices of white onion.

Separate the endive leaves and cut them into medium-sized pieces. Lay them in a salad bowl. Peel and section the oranges; carefully remove any seeds and all the white membrane surrounding each segment. Lay the segments on top of the endive. Sprinkle the almonds over the top.

In a small bowl stir together the lemon juice, orange juice, cream and salt and cayenne pepper to taste until well mixed. Pour the dressing over the salad and serve immediately.

Serves 4

Two-Color Salad

1½ cups (6 oz/185 g) shelled peas
¼ lb (100 g) green beans, trimmed
2 carrots, about 6 oz (185 g) total
   weight, peeled and cut into long,
   thin strips
2 zucchini (courgettes), about 6 oz
   (185 g) total weight, cut into small
   cubes
1 tablespoon dry white wine
1 tablespoon tarragon vinegar
2 tablespoons heavy whipping
   (double) cream
2 tablespoons sunflower seed oil
salt

This salad of cooked vegetables can be enjoyed warm or cold. Delicate and slightly sweet, it goes well with meats, fish or cheeses. If you like, mayonnaise (recipe on page 13) flavored with fresh mint and chives can be used in place of the cream dressing.

*A*rrange the peas and beans on a steamer rack, place over a pan of boiling water, cover and steam for 5 minutes. Add the carrots and steam for 2–3 minutes longer. Then add the zucchini and steam until all the vegetables are tender, a few minutes longer. Transfer to a serving plate.

   Meanwhile, in a small bowl mix together the wine, vinegar, cream, oil and salt to taste until well blended. Pour over the vegetables and serve.

Serves 4

Butter Lettuce and Tarragon Salad

2 small heads butter lettuce, separated into leaves
2 tablespoons minced fresh tarragon
2 tablespoons minced fresh chives
1 tablespoon red wine vinegar
1 tablespoon Dijon mustard
salt
¼ cup (2 fl oz/60 ml) extra-virgin olive oil

Fresh and light, this salad makes a nice side dish to fish or meat. If it is to accompany fish, substitute lemon juice for the vinegar. Slices of hard-cooked egg are an attractive garnish. Minced basil and flat-leaf (Italian) parsley can be added to the dressing, if you wish.

Discard the largest and darkest lettuce leaves; use only the most tender ones. If the leaves are large, tear them into pieces. Arrange in a salad bowl and sprinkle with the tarragon and chives.

In a small bowl stir together the vinegar, mustard and salt to taste until well mixed. Add the oil and stir vigorously with a fork until blended. Pour the dressing over the lettuce, toss well and serve.

Serves 4

Zucchini and Mint Salad

8 baby zucchini (courgettes), about
 ¾ lb (400 g) total weight
2 tablespoons fresh lemon juice
1 tablespoon finely minced fresh mint
 leaves
salt
cayenne pepper
¼ cup (2 fl oz/60 ml) extra-virgin
 olive oil

It is important to use very young, tender zucchini in this salad. The result will be a delicate and refreshing flavor that complements omelets, fish or fresh cheeses. Flat-leaf (Italian) parsley can be used in place of the mint.

Fill a bowl with water and ice cubes, add the zucchini and refrigerate for a couple of hours. (This makes the zucchini crunchy and easier to cut.)

   Drain the zucchini and dry well, then cut crosswise into very thin slices. Arrange the slices on a serving plate.

   In a small bowl stir together the lemon juice, mint and salt and cayenne pepper to taste until well mixed. Add the oil and stir vigorously until blended. Pour the dressing over the zucchini and serve.

Serves 4

Grapefruit and Olive Salad with Red Leaf Lettuce

1 head red leaf lettuce, separated into
   leaves
2 grapefruits
12 black olives, pitted
2 tablespoons strong-flavored mustard
1 teaspoon cider vinegar
1 teaspoon sugar
salt
white pepper
¼ cup (2 fl oz/60 ml) extra-virgin
   olive oil

A tasty salad that goes well with chicken or fish. Select an aromatic, pleasantly pungent mustard flavored with spices and other seasonings for the dressing. In the colder months the salad can be made heartier with the addition of cooked beets, red cabbage, red (Spanish) onion and some pomegranate seeds.

If the lettuce leaves are large, tear them into pieces. Place in a salad bowl. Peel and section the grapefruits; carefully remove all the white membrane surrounding each segment and any seeds. Add to the lettuce along with the olives.

   In a small bowl stir together the mustard, vinegar, sugar and salt and white pepper to taste until well mixed. Add the oil and stir vigorously until blended. Pour the dressing over the salad, toss well and serve.

Serves 4

Orange and Date Fruit Salad

4 oranges
2 bananas, peeled and sliced crosswise
12 dates, pitted and halved lengthwise
3 tablespoons honey
juice of 2 lemons
1 teaspoon ground cinnamon

A simple and flavorful mélange. Chopped pistachios or hazelnuts (filberts) can be strewn over the top.

*P*eel the oranges, carefully removing all the white membrane. Cut crosswise into thin slices and remove any seeds. Arrange on a serving dish. Top with the banana slices and then with the date halves.

In a small bowl stir together the honey and lemon juice until well mixed. Add the cinnamon and stir well, then pour evenly over the fruit. Cover and refrigerate for about 2 hours before serving.

Serves 4

Berry and Banana Salad

½ lb (250 g) strawberries, stemmed
 and thinly sliced lengthwise
½ lb (250 g) blueberries
2 bananas, peeled and thinly sliced
¾ cup (4 oz/120 g) confectioners'
 (icing) sugar
juice of 1 orange
juice of ½ lemon

Wild berries picked in the woods are the most fragrant, and it is best to wash them with a little white wine instead of water, to preserve their perfume. This salad can also be dressed with white wine and sugar, or cream and sugar.

Combine the berries and bananas in a salad bowl. In a small bowl stir together the sugar and the orange and lemon juices until the sugar dissolves. Pour the dressing over the fruit and serve.

Serves 4

White Wine Peach Salad

6 white peaches, peeled, pitted and cut lengthwise into thin slices
1 cup (5 oz/150 g) confectioners' (icing) sugar
2 cups (16 fl oz/500 ml) dry white wine

The white peaches called for in this recipe have a more delicate perfume than the common yellow variety. In wintertime, use red wine in place of white, and substitute apples or pears for the peaches. These winter fruits will need to be simmered in the red wine–sugar mixture over low heat until they are tender, about 10 minutes; cool before serving. They do not, however, need to be refrigerated.

Place the peaches in a salad bowl. In a separate bowl, stir together the sugar and wine until the sugar is thoroughly dissolved. Pour the dressing over the peaches, cover and refrigerate for at least 1 hour or for up to 12 hours before serving.

Serves 4

Fresh Fruit Salad in Melon Boat

1 cantaloupe
2 peaches, peeled if desired
6 apricots, peeled if desired
1 small bunch seedless grapes, about
   6 oz (185 g), stemmed
2 tablespoons confectioners' (icing)
   sugar
juice of 1 orange
juice of 1 lemon
thin strips lemon zest for garnish

Use only the finest seasonal fruits for this striking salad. Cherries, strawberries, figs, mangoes and pears can be added to or substituted for the fruits listed here. For a richer dressing, add light (single) cream in place of the orange and lemon juices.

Cut off about 2 inches (5 cm) of the stem end of the melon. Remove the seeds and discard. Scoop out the flesh into small balls and place in a bowl. Refrigerate the carved-out melon boat.

Pit the peaches and apricots and cut them into thin slices or cubes. Add them to the bowl holding the melon balls, along with the grapes. Sieve the sugar over the top and then sprinkle with the orange and lemon juices. Stir well.

Spoon the fruit mixture into the melon boat and decorate with lemon zest. Serve immediately or chill for 30 minutes before serving.

Serves 4

Glossary

The following glossary defines terms specifically as they relate to salads, including major and unusual ingredients and basic techniques.

ANCHOVIES
Tiny saltwater fish, related to sardines; most often found as canned fillets that have been salted and preserved in oil. Imported anchovy fillets packed in olive oil are the most commonly available; those packed in salt, available canned in some Italian delicatessens, are considered the finest.

ARTICHOKES
Also known as globe artichokes. The large flower buds of a type of thistle, grown primarily in the Mediterranean and in California. The tightly packed cluster of tough, pointed, prickly leaves conceal tender, gray-green flesh at the vegetable's center—the heart.

BASIL
Sweet, spicy herb popular in Italian and French cooking, particularly as a seasoning for tomatoes and tomato sauces.

BEANS, BORLOTTI
Italian variety of medium-sized dried beans, kidney shaped with pink or beige skins speckled in burgundy. Available in Italian delicatessens and specialty-food shops. Substitute pink kidney beans or pinto beans.

BEANS, NAVY
Small, white, thin-skinned, oval dried beans. Widely available in supermarkets. Also known as Boston beans. Great Northern beans may be substituted.

BELL PEPPER
Fresh, sweet-fleshed, bell-shaped member of the pepper family. Also known as capsicum. Most common in the unripe green form, although ripened red or yellow varieties are also available. Creamy pale-yellow, orange and purple-black types may also be found.

To prepare a raw bell pepper, begin by cutting it in half vertically with a sharp knife. Pull out the stem section from each half, along with the cluster of seeds attached to it. Remove any remaining seeds, along with any thin white ribs to which they are attached. Cut the pepper halves into quarters, strips or thin slices, as called for in individual recipes.

BROCCOLI
Member of the cabbage family, usually green to purple-green in color, characterized by tightly clustered flowers—known as florets—growing at the end of sturdy stalks. The florets are the most tender part, but the stems, if thickly peeled, are also good to eat. Available year-round.

CAPERS
Small, pickled buds of a bush common to the Mediterranean; used whole as a savory flavoring or garnish.

CAYENNE PEPPER
Very hot ground spice derived from dried cayenne chili peppers.

CHICKEN, SMOKED
Sold in specialty-food stores and delicatessens, smoked chicken has a sweet, mildly smoky flavor and tender texture that emphasize the natural qualities of the chicken.

CHICK-PEAS
Also known as garbanzo beans. Tan dried beans similar in shape to a small hazelnut (filbert), with a firm, slightly dry texture and mildly nutlike flavor.

CHIVES
Mild, sweet herb with a flavor reminiscent of the **onion**, to which it is related. Although chives are available dried in the herb-and-spice section of a supermarket, fresh chives possess the best flavor.

CREAM
The terms *light* and *heavy* describe cream's butterfat content and related richness. Light cream, not available everywhere under this name, has a butterfat level varying from 18–30 percent. It is sometimes called coffee cream or table cream. Heavy whipping cream, sometimes simply labeled heavy cream, has a butterfat content of at least 36 percent. For the best flavor and cooking properties, purchase fresh cream, avoiding long-lasting varieties that have been processed by ultraheat methods. Light cream is also known as single cream; in Britain, use double cream for heavy cream.

CUMIN
Middle Eastern spice with a strong, dusky, aromatic flavor, popular in cuisines of its region of origin

along with those of Latin America, India and parts of Europe. Sold either ground or as whole, small, crescent-shaped seeds.

CURRY POWDER
Generic term for blends of spices commonly used to flavor East Indian–style dishes. Most curry powders will include coriander, **cumin**, chili powder, fenugreek and turmeric; other additions may include cardamom, cinnamon, cloves, allspice, **fennel** seeds and ginger. Best purchased in small quantities, because flavor diminishes rapidly after opening.

DILL
Herb with fine, feathery leaves and sweet, aromatic flavor well suited to pickling brines, vegetables, seafood, chicken, veal and pork. Sold fresh or dried.

FENNEL
Crisp, refreshing, mildly anise-flavored bulb vegetable, sometimes called by its Italian name, *finocchio*. Also valued for its fine, feathery leaves, which are used as a fresh or dried herb, and for its small, crescent-shaped seeds, dried and used as a spice.

FIG
Summer fruit characterized by its many tiny edible seeds, its sweet, slightly astringent flavor and its very soft, succulent texture.

GARLIC
Pungent bulb popular worldwide as a flavoring ingredient, both raw and cooked. For the best flavor,

GELATIN

Unflavored commercial gelatin gives delicate body to molded salads. Sold in ¼-oz (7-g) envelopes, each of which is sufficient to jell about 2 cups (16 fl oz/ 500 ml) liquid.

To unmold a gelatin salad once it has set, carefully run a knife tip around the edge of the salad inside the mold. Then dip the mold, almost to the top, into a bowl of hot water for a few seconds.

Place the serving plate over the top of the mold, making sure it fits snugly against the mold. With both hands, firmly hold the plate and mold together.

Swiftly invert and give them one sharp, slight downward shake to help dislodge the salad. Carefully lift off the mold. If the salad does not unmold, repeat the procedure from the first step.

purchase whole heads of dry garlic in the supermarket vegetable department, separating individual cloves from the head as needed; it is best not to purchase more than you will use in 1 or 2 weeks, as garlic can shrivel and lose its flavor with prolonged storage. To peel a garlic clove, place on a work surface and cover with the side of a large chef's knife. Press down firmly but carefully on the side of the knife to crush the clove slightly; the dry skin will then slip off easily.

GOAT CHEESE

Most cheeses made from goat's milk are fresh and creamy, with a distinctively sharp tang; they are sold shaped into small rounds, about 2 inches (5 cm) in diameter, or logs 1–2 inches (2.5–5 cm) in diameter and 4–6 inches (10–15 cm) long. Some goat cheeses are coated with mixtures of herbs, with pepper, or with ash, which mildly flavors them. Also known by the French term *chèvre*.

HONEY

The natural, sweet, syruplike substance produced by bees from flower nectar, honey subtly reflects the color, taste and aroma of the blossoms from which it was made. Milder varieties, such as clover and orange blossom, are lighter in color and better suited to general cooking purposes.

HORSERADISH

Pungent, hot-tasting root, a member of the mustard family, sold fresh and whole, or already grated and bottled as a prepared sauce. The best prepared horseradish is the freshly grated variety, bottled in a light vinegar and found in the refrigerated section of the supermarket.

MINT

Refreshing, sweet herb used fresh to flavor lamb, vegetables and fruits.

MOZZARELLA

Rindless white, mild-tasting Italian variety of cheese traditionally made from water buffalo's milk and sold fresh. Commercially produced and packaged cow's milk mozzarella is now much more common, although it has less flavor. Look for fresh mozzarella sold immersed in water.

MUSTARD, COARSE-GRAINED AND DIJON

Dijon mustard is made in Dijon, France, from dark brown mustard seeds (unless otherwise marked *blanc*) and white wine or wine vinegar. Pale in color, fairly hot and sharp tasting, true Dijon mustard and non-French blends labeled "Dijon-style" are widely available in supermarkets and specialty-food stores. Coarse-grained mustards, which have a granular texture due to roughly ground mustard seeds, include the French *moutarde de Meaux* and a number of high-quality British and German varieties.

OIL, OLIVE

Extra-virgin olive oil, extracted from olives on the first pressing without use of heat or chemicals, is preferred for salads. Many brands, varying in color and strength of flavor, are now available; choose one that suits your taste. The higher-priced extra-virgin olive oils usually are

of better quality. Store in an airtight container away from heat and light.

OIL, PEANUT

Pale-gold oil with a subtle hint of the peanut's richness. Used in cooking and for salad dressings.

OIL, SESAME

Oil pressed from sesame seeds, which impart to it their nutlike flavor. Asian sesame oil from China or Japan is made with toasted seeds, resulting in a dark reddish-brown color and very rich, aromatic flavor; it is used primarily as a seasoning. Pale, cold-pressed sesame oil, available in health-food stores, is good for salad dressings.

OIL, SUNFLOWER SEED

Pale, relatively flavorless oil used in dressings and for cooking.

OLIVES, BLACK

Throughout Mediterranean Europe, black olives are cured in various combinations of salt, seasonings, brines, vinegars and oils to produce a range of pungently flavored results. Good-quality cured olives are available in ethnic delicatessens, specialty-food shops and well-stocked supermarkets.

ONION, GREEN

Variety of onion harvested immature, leaves and all, before its bulb has formed. Green and white parts may both be enjoyed, raw or cooked, for their mild but still pronounced onion flavor. Also called spring onion or scallion.

OREGANO

Aromatic, pungent and spicy Mediterranean herb—also known as wild marjoram—used fresh or dried as a seasoning for all kinds of savory dishes. Especially popular with tomatoes and other vegetables.

PARMESAN
Hard, thick-crusted Italian cheese with a sharp, salty, full flavor resulting from at least 2 years of aging. Buy in block form, to grate or shave fresh as needed. The finest of the many Italian varieties is parmigiano-reggiano.

PARSLEY, CURLY-LEAF
Most common form of the popular herb in the United States, usually used as a garnish.

PARSLEY, FLAT-LEAF
Variety of the popular fresh herb with broad, flat leaves that have a more pronounced flavor than the common curly-leafed type. Also called Italian parsley.

PEACH, WHITE
Variety of the summer fruit with a pale yellow, almost white flesh. More common yellow peaches may be substituted.

PEPPERCORNS
Pepper, the most common of all savory spices, is best purchased as whole peppercorns, to be ground in a pepper mill as needed, or coarsely crushed. Pungent black peppercorns derive from slightly underripe pepper berries, whose hulls oxidize as they dry. Milder white peppercorns come from fully ripened berries, with the husks removed before drying. Sharp-tasting unripened green peppercorns are sold in water, pickled in brine or dried.

PINE NUTS
Small, ivory-colored seeds extracted from the cones of a species of pine tree, with a rich, slightly resinous flavor. Used

SALAD GREENS
An ever-greater range of salad leaves is becoming available at supermarkets and greengrocers, ready to add a wide variety of colors, shapes, tastes and textures to the salad bowl. Those shown here are among the most common; other choices include oak leaf, red leaf and iceberg lettuces; red and white cabbage; Chinese (nappa) cabbage; and dandelion greens, escarole, kale, sorrel and Swiss chard (silverbeet).

Arugula Slender, multiple-lobed leaves with a peppery, slightly bitter flavor. Also known as rocket.

Belgian Endive Refreshing, slightly bitter spear-shaped leaves, white to pale yellow green—or sometimes red—tightly packed in cylindrical heads 4–6 inches (10–15 cm) long. Also known as chicory or witloof.

Butter Lettuce Relatively small type of round lettuce with soft, loosely packed, tender, mildly flavored leaves. Also known as Boston lettuce. Butter lettuce is a member of the butterhead

family, which also includes the Bibb, or limestone, variety.

Chicory A relative of Belgian endive, with loosely packed, curly leaves characterized by their bitter flavor. The paler center leaves, or heart, of a head of chicory are milder-tasting than the dark-green outer leaves. Also called curly endive.

Green Leaf Lettuce Any of a variety of loose-leafed lettuces characterized by their slightly crinkled, medium- to dark-green leaves and by a flavor more pronounced than Bibb or butter lettuces.

Radicchio Leaf vegetable related to Belgian endive. The most common variety has a spherical head, reddish purple leaves with creamy white ribs, and a mildly bitter flavor. Other varieties are slightly tapered and vary a bit in color. Also called red chicory.

Romaine Lettuce Popular variety of lettuce with elongated, pale-green leaves characterized by their crisp texture and slightly pungent flavor. Also called cos lettuce.

Savoy Cabbage Flavorful variety of round cabbage with attractive, tightly packed leaves patterned with a lacelike network of veins.

Spinach Choose smaller, more tender spinach leaves for salads. Be sure to wash thoroughly, in several changes of water, to eliminate all dirt and sand.

Watercress Refreshing, slightly peppery, dark-green leaf vegetable commercially cultivated and also found wild in freshwater streams.

whole as an ingredient or garnish, or puréed as a thickener. Also known by the Italian *pinoli*.

RADISH

Crisp root vegetable, usually eaten raw and prized for its refreshing flavor characterized by a pungent, peppery hotness that varies from mild to assertive depending upon the variety.

SPROUTS

Small, immature shoots sprouted from a wide variety of seeds and beans. Among the most popular, illustrated here, are delicate, mild-tasting alfalfa sprouts (top) and larger, crisp and succulent mung bean sprouts.

SUGAR, CONFECTIONERS'

Finely pulverized form of sugar, also known as powdered or icing sugar, which dissolves very quickly. To prevent it from absorbing moisture in the air and caking, the sugar includes some cornstarch.

TARRAGON

Fragrant, distinctively sweet herb used fresh or dried as a classic seasoning for salads, chicken, light meats, seafood and eggs.

THYME

Fragrant, clean-tasting, small-leaved herb popular fresh or dried as a seasoning for salads, poultry, light meats, seafood or vegetables.

TOMATO

During summer, when tomatoes are in season, use the best red or yellow sun-ripened tomatoes you can find. At other times of year, plum tomatoes, sometimes called Roma or egg tomatoes, are likely to have the best flavor and texture for salads.

To peel fresh tomatoes, first bring a saucepan of water to a boil. Using a small, sharp knife, cut out the core from the stem end of the tomato. Then cut a shallow X in the skin at the tomato's base. Submerge for about 20 seconds in the boiling water, then remove and dip in a bowl of cold water. Starting at the X, peel the skin from the tomato, using your fingertips and, if necessary, the knife blade. Cut the tomatoes in half and turn each half cut-side down. Then cut as directed in individual recipes.

WORCESTERSHIRE SAUCE

Traditional English seasoning or condiment; an intensely flavorful, savory and aromatic blend of many ingredients, including molasses, soy sauce, **garlic, onion** and **anchovies.** Popular as a seasoning, marinade ingredient or table sauce.

YOGURT, PLAIN

Milk fermented by bacterial cultures that impart a mildly acidic flavor and custardlike texture. So-called plain yogurt simply refers to the unflavored product, to distinguish it from the

VINEGARS

Literally "sour" wine, vinegar results when certain strains of yeast cause wine—or some other alcoholic liquid such as apple cider or Japanese rice wine—to ferment for a second time, turning it acidic.

The best-quality wine vinegars begin with good-quality wine. Red wine vinegar, like the wine from which it is made, has a more robust flavor than vinegar produced from white wine. Balsamic vinegar, a specialty of Modena, Italy, is a vinegar made from reduced grape juice aged for many years. Flavored vinegars are made with herbs such as tarragon and dill or with fruits such as raspberries.

Make your own flavored vinegars by placing your favorite herb or spice—or onion or garlic—in a bottle of vinegar and allowing it to steep for at least several days. Remove and discard the flavorings before use.

many popular varieties of flavored and sweetened yogurt. Available made from whole, low-fat or nonfat milk; for salad dressings, low-fat plain yogurt is the best choice.

ZEST

Thin, brightly colored, outermost layer of a citrus fruit's peel, containing most of its aromatic essential oils—a lively source of flavor. Zest may be removed with a simple tool known as a zester, drawn across the fruit's skin to remove the zest in thin strips; with a fine hand-held grater; or in wide strips with a vegetable peeler or a paring knife held almost parallel to the fruit's skin. Zest removed with the latter two tools may then be thinly sliced or chopped on a cutting board.

ZUCCHINI, BABY

Small, immature form—measuring no more than 3–5 inches (7.5–12 cm) long—of the tender, tube-shaped relative of squash, sometimes referred to as summer squash or courgette; with edible green, yellow or green-and-cream-striped skin and pale, tender flesh. Small zucchini have a finer texture and flavor, and less pronounced seeds, than fully matured specimens. They are sometimes sold with their delicate, edible blossoms still attached.

Index

ACKNOWLEDGMENTS

The publishers would like to thank the following people and organizations for their
generous assistance and support in producing this book:
Lorenza de' Medici, Amy Morton, Ken DellaPenta, Sharon-Ann C. Lott,
Stephen W. Griswold, the buyers for Gardener's Eden, and the buyers and store
managers for Pottery Barn and Williams-Sonoma stores.

The following kindly lent props for the photography: Biordi Art Imports, Fillamento,
Galisteo, Stephanie Greenleigh; Sue Fisher King, Lorraine & Judson Puckett,
Gianfranco Savio, Sue White and Chuck Williams.